BERLIN
AND
POTSDAM

Text: Bernhard Schneidewind · **Translation:** KERN AG, Sprachendienste
Concept and Design: N. Arndt, R. Dohrmann, B. Nuske
Photos: Picture archive Preußischer Kulturbesitz (J. Liepe, M. Galli, F. Profitlich, K. Göken, J. P. Anders), blumebild.com, R. Carow, Deutsche Luftbild, Deutsche Presseagentur, U. Findeisen, W. Freimark, S. Gödecke, Handrick, imago, N. Krüger, T. Krüger, F. Kübler, U. Latza, Lehnartz-Fotografie, Dirk Laubner/Berlin, Maecke/Laif/G.A.F.F., W. Okon, W. Otto, A. Pulwey, S. Rehberg, D. Scherf, G. Schneider, Schöning picture, E. Schröder, V. Vollmer, H. Wanke, W. Weber, Wikipedia, picture alliance/A. Burgi
We'd like to thank the following institutions for their friendly support and cooperation:
Prussian Palace and Gardens Foundation Berlin-Brandenburg,
DDR Museum Berlin, Deutsche Entertainment AG - DEAG
Cartography: Pharus-Verlag, M. Goldenbaum
Editors: R. Dohrmann a. N. Arndt

SCHÖNING VERLAG

Distribution: SCHIKKUS · Nordlichtstraße 71 · 13405 Berlin ·Tel. 030/36 40 77-0
Internet: www.schikkus.de · Email: info@schikkus.de
Overall conception and © Copyright by
SCHÖNING GmbH & CO KG
An der Hülshorst 5 · 23568 LÜBECK
Fon (04 51) 310 3-0 · Fax (04 51) 3 52 83
Email: info@schoening-verlag.de
Internet: www.schoening-verlag.de
ISBN: 978-3-89917-369-7
7. Auflage

Metropolis or Province?

Berlin is not unique. Worldwide, there are around 40 places called Berlin, Berlin, each with an independent administration. Without a doubt, the Berlin situated on the rivers Spree and Havel is the biggest Berlin in the world. Yet it is not the oldest. Berlin in the municipality of Seedorf in the Schleswig-Holstein district of Segeberg, received its first documented mention in 1215. The Berlin, which is now the biggest one and which often likes to boast that it is also the greatest, only received its first – rather questionable –

documented mention in 1237 and its first proper one seven years later. There is reason to believe that the Berlin calendar started in the year 1237 because the National Socialists needed a reason for a mammoth celebration a year after the German success during the Olympic Games of 1936: the 700-year anniversary.

The meaning of the name is unclear for all Berlins of this world. The Slavic root "brlo" or "berlo" meaning bog, swamp, or humid place, is considered the most likely origin. Experts are not even 50% certain. However, the assumption that the name stems from the Ascanian Margrave Albrecht "der Bär" (The Bear) is just as wrong as finding the proof of this wild guess in the fact the bear is the Berlin's heraldic animal.

But all that is very fitting for the city of Berlin. It is a beast. This city has repeatedly devoured its own mothers and fathers. It never brought any ruler, king, emperor, despot or chancellor any lasting good fortune. Somehow, sooner or later, it always came to an end. And subsequently, Berlin always had to redefine itself again and again. This mostly happened with a radicalness that made outsiders swoon. "It's not all that easy to define

the reputation of or life in a city that's constantly on the move, constantly on the brink of change, never resting in its yesterday", Flâneur Franz Hessel wrote in the 1920s. That still applies today.

Yesterday – that refers to the Hohenzollerns, who received the little patches of land called Cölln and Berlin on opposite sides of the river Spree from Emperor Sigismund in 1415. It was not a generous gift; it was actually more of a misery. The land was swampy, untouched by the kind of culture which already existed in the southern parts of Europe at the time. Over five centuries, the Hohenzollerns nurtured this spot

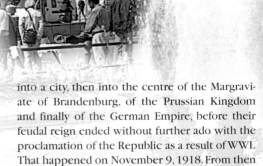

into a city, then into the centre of the Margraviate of Brandenburg, of the Prussian Kingdom and finally of the German Empire, before their feudal reign ended without further ado with the proclamation of the Republic as a result of WWI. That happened on November 9, 1918. From then on, Berlin and the entire German Reich were

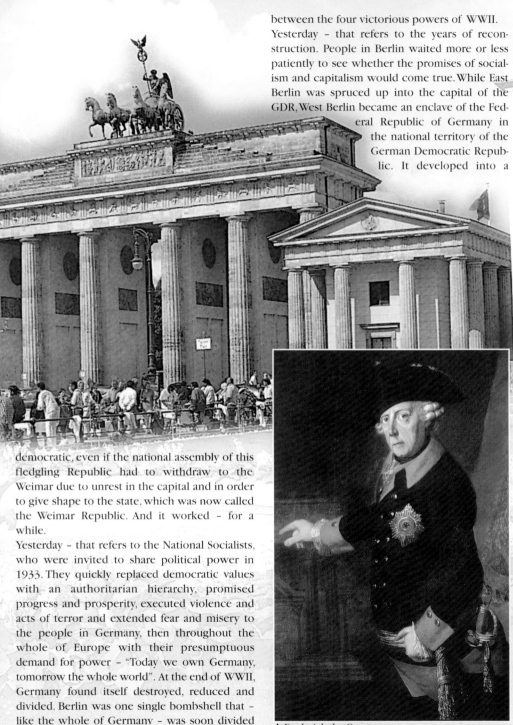

between the four victorious powers of WWII. Yesterday – that refers to the years of reconstruction. People in Berlin waited more or less patiently to see whether the promises of socialism and capitalism would come true. While East Berlin was spruced up into the capital of the GDR, West Berlin became an enclave of the Federal Republic of Germany in the national territory of the German Democratic Republic. It developed into a

democratic, even if the national assembly of this fledgling Republic had to withdraw to the Weimar due to unrest in the capital and in order to give shape to the state, which was now called the Weimar Republic. And it worked – for a while.

Yesterday – that refers to the National Socialists, who were invited to share political power in 1933. They quickly replaced democratic values with an authoritarian hierarchy, promised progress and prosperity, executed violence and acts of terror and extended fear and misery to the people in Germany, then throughout the whole of Europe with their presumptuous demand for power – "Today we own Germany, tomorrow the whole world". At the end of WWII, Germany found itself destroyed, reduced and divided. Berlin was one single bombshell that – like the whole of Germany – was soon divided

▲ Frederick the Great

3

▲ The Stadtschloss (City Palace) around 1880

world of glamour, vamped up by copious amounts of subsidies and aid money; it was meant to serve as a "showcase of the West".

Yesterday – that refers to the construction of a monstrous Wall right through Berlin, which was intended to render any exits from the GDR and entries from the other side impossible. This piece of architecture, constantly repaired and improved on, was maintained for 28 years, before it was torn down completely peacefully overnight – something that people on both sides of the Wall had not thought possible. On that November 9, 1989, Berlin became one city again. Many people in Berlin still cannot quite believe

it. The inner-city border is gone, yet it still exists, more or less solidly, in people's minds. A resident of Charlottenburg who wants to get to the "Alex", goes into "the East", although Alexanderplatz is located in the city centre district "Mitte". A resident of Pankowe travelling to Neukölln goes into "the West", although Neukölln is a district in the south-east of the city. Did something absolute manifest itself in people's heads in over those 40 years when the city was divided? Or is it only a new version of the Berliners' "Kiez" (neighbourhood) identity that has always existed?

Greater Berlin, which was almost identical to the city as it is today, was founded in 1920 by the incorporation of seven city districts, 59 country municipalities and 27 estates. If you ask Berliners where they live, they will insist first on their district, and only then on Berlin as a whole, maybe. So people from, say, Spandau, continue to go into the "city", when they visit the centre of Berlin. The centre is surrounded by many sub-centres. While tourists predominantly stick to the city centre, be it City-West around the Gedächtniskirche (Memorial Church) or the city centre around Alexanderplatz, life of people constantly living in Berlin mainly happens in the sub-centres. One only goes to the city centre with outside visitors, really. For the requirements of everyday life, it is enough to live near e.g. Schlossstraße in Steglitz, Müllerstraße in Wedding, Frankfurter Allee in Friedrichshain, Wilmersdorfer Straße in Charlottenburg, Berliner Allee in Weißensee, Karl-Marx-Straße in Neukölln or Tempelhofer Damm in Tempelhof.

Anywhere in Berlin is "Kiez". This does not make the eternal discussion about whether the city is a metropolis or still a province, any easier. Nobody wants to be provincial, but nearly everyone is a villager. That includes those who do not have a generation buried on a graveyard already. In Prenzlauer Berg you could get the impression that the Swabian accent is obligatory, in Kreuzberg you might think whole Anatolian villages had found their new habitat in some streets.

So what is Berlin really?

Full of crap, some might say. Some consider Berlin to be "constructed, fabricated, not born; it was there before it was pregnant with itself, a child before the mother", the travel writer William Hausenstein wrote last century. "Poor but sexy", a Governing Mayor once called it and thus defiantly as well as wantonly combined two characteristics, which do not seem to fit together at all.

Maybe it is precisely this high-spiritedness that marks the city. Some things here were and still are unbelievable and impudent at the same time. For example, there is the story about the pathological miser, the "Soldier King" Frederick William I of Prussia, father of Frederick the Great, who founded Berlin's oyster culture. "There were only two things", according to city chronicler Walter Kiaulehn, "that were stronger than his stinginess: his need to constantly wash his hands and his greed for oysters. His handwashing eccentricity made him to install water pipes in the 700 rooms and halls of the Berlin Palace and because of his greed for oysters, he had an extra mail route installed, Berlin-Hamburg-Berlin, on which horse-drawn carriages stocked with ice constantly travelled back and forth between Hamburg and Berlin. The Berliners also benefited from this oyster mail service. Prussia owned its own oyster banks in Danish

▲ William I.

▲ William II.

waters, and these 'fiscal oysters', as they were called, were small but especially tasty... and on top of that cheap.

So is it any wonder that the food department in the giant store KaDeWe – it is considered the most sophisticated in Europe – and is also frequented by rubbish collectors in their bright orange work clothes at lunchtime? Bockwurst simply tastes better here. "Weita nüscht. Watt dajejen?" as the Berliners would say – "That's just that. Got a problem with it?"

Timeline

Around 720 – First Slavic settlements on the rivers Havel and Spree

993 – First mention of Potsdam

1197 – First documented mention of Spandau

▲ The Reichstag around 1900

1209 – First documented entry of Köpenick

1237 – First entry about Cölln

1244 – First documented mention of Berlin

1308 – Berlin and Cölln conclude a defense pact

1359 – Berlin and Cölln join the Hanseatic League

1432 – Joint administration of

1442 – Planning commences for a palace by the river Spree around

1450 – Around 8,000 people live in Berlin-Cölln

1486 – Berlin-Cölln becomes permanent seat of the Hohenzollern family

1539 – Elector Johannes II. converts to Protestantism

1600 – Berlin counts 12,000 inhabitants

1660 – Beginning of the extension of Potsdam as Royal Residence

1685 – The edict of Potsdam attracts many Huguenots to Berlin

1696 – Opening of the Academy of the Arts

1701 – Frederick I is crowned first King of Prussia

1713 – Potsdam is constructed into a garrison town

1733 – In Potsdam building works for the "second new part of town" start with the Dutch Quarter

1745 – Building works commences for Sanssouci Palace

1760 – Population of Berlin now exceeds 100,000

1810 – Foundation of the Berlin University

1830 – 247,500 people live in Berlin

1838 – Opening of the train line Berlin-Potsdam

1844 – Opening of Zoologischer Garten

1850 – Inauguration of the church St. Nikolaikirche in Potsdam (first 1837)

1871 – Berlin becomes capital of the German Reich

1880 – Population amounts to around 1,122 330

1882 – Opening of the first urban railway line

1902 – Launch of the first underground railway line

1910 – Population amounts to around 2,071 257

1918 – Proclamation of the Republic (9.11.1918)

1920 – Incorporation of seven towns, 59 country municipalities and 27 estates to make up Greater Berlin. Population around 3,858 393.

1921 – Opening of the automobile, transport and test route (Avus)

1926 – Inauguration of the Radio Tower

1930 – Opening of the Pergamon Museum

▲ Destroyed Reichstag 1945

6

1933 – Adolf Hitler (NSDAP) named Reich Chancellor

1936 – Summer Olympic Games

1939 – Start of WWII with the German Reich's descent on Poland

1940 – Population amounts to 4,354 087

▲ Brandenburg Gate in the 1950s

▲ Airlift Memorial

1999 – The German Bundestag moves from Bonn to Berlin

2006 – 3,395 189 people live in Berlin, including 466,518 foreigners from 183 nations. Coordinates: 52°31' N and 13°24' E. The longitude equals that of Napels, the latitude equals London's. The average height above NN amounts to 34 meters, the highest peaks are the Müggel mountains at 115 meters.

Area: 888 square kilometres, including around 40 percent green space. The city limits have a circumference of 229 kilometres, the biggest East-West extension amounts to 45 kilometres, North-South 38 kilometres.

1942 – Wannsee Conference decides on the systematic murder of Jews in Europe

1945 – Capitulation of the German Reich The Potsdam Agreement between the four major wartime Allies establishes the division of the city into four sectors

1946 – Population amounts to approx. 2,800 000

1948/ 1949 – Blockade of the Western sectors of the city by the Soviet Union – Berlin Airlift

1949 – Foundation of the Federal Republic of Germany and the German Democratic Republic

1953 – Workers' revolt in Berlin and the whole GDR

1961 – Construction of the Wall around the Western sectors of the city

1969 – Opening of the Television Tower at Alexanderplatz

1980 – Population amounts to 3,150 729. 1,998 200 (West Berlin) and 1,152 529 (East Berlin)

1989 – Reunification of the city following the fall of the Wall. Glienicke bridge between Berlin and Potsdam is reopened

1990 – Population amounts to 3,329 300

1991 – Berlin declared capital of the reunified Germany

▲ Fall of the Wall in 1989

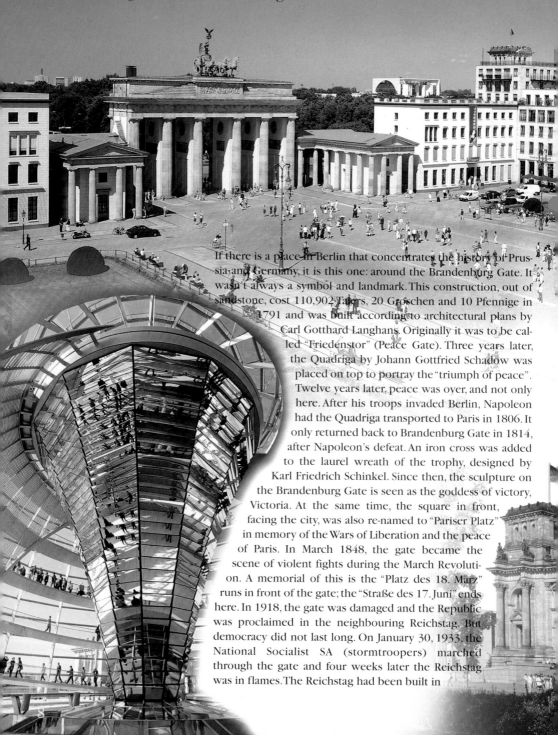

Brandenburg Gate and Reichstag

If there is a place in Berlin that concentrates the history of Prussia and Germany, it is this one: around the Brandenburg Gate. It wasn't always a symbol and landmark. This construction, out of sandstone, cost 110,902 Talers, 20 Groschen and 10 Pfennige in 1791 and was built according to architectural plans by Carl Gotthard Langhans. Originally it was to be called "Friedenstor" (Peace Gate). Three years later, the Quadriga by Johann Gottfried Schadow was placed on top to portray the "triumph of peace". Twelve years later, peace was over, and not only here. After his troops invaded Berlin, Napoleon had the Quadriga transported to Paris in 1806. It only returned back to Brandenburg Gate in 1814, after Napoleon's defeat. An iron cross was added to the laurel wreath of the trophy, designed by Karl Friedrich Schinkel. Since then, the sculpture on the Brandenburg Gate is seen as the goddess of victory, Victoria. At the same time, the square in front, facing the city, was also re-named to "Pariser Platz" in memory of the Wars of Liberation and the peace of Paris. In March 1848, the gate became the scene of violent fights during the March Revolution. A memorial of this is the "Platz des 18. März" runs in front of the gate; the "Straße des 17. Juni" ends here. In 1918, the gate was damaged and the Republic was proclaimed in the neighbouring Reichstag. But democracy did not last long. On January 30, 1933, the National Socialist SA (stormtroopers) marched through the gate and four weeks later the Reichstag was in flames. The Reichstag had been built in

▲ The Quadriga on top of the Brandenburg Gate

1884-94 according to plans by the Architect Paul Wallot in the Italian High Renaissance style of the so-called Gründerzeit (period of promoterism). In 1882, Emperor William II laid the foundation stone for the colossal building, which cost around 30 million gold marks. During WWI, the dedication "Dem Deutschen Volke" (To the German people) was added above the entrance. On November 9, 1918, Philip Scheidemann proclaimed the Republic from an upstairs window. In the badly damaged and partially restored building, the German Bundestag has met here from 1970 onwards. After Berlin became German capital again in 1991 following reunification, the Reichstag was renovated and extended according to plans by the British Architect Sir Norman Foster. In 1999, it was ceremoniously inaugurated again. The giant glass dome is spectacular. The Brandenburg Gate used to be a symbol of the undecided "German question". On November 9, 70 years after the proclamation of the first German Republic, this question was answered and the Brandenburg Gate was re-opened. Today, both gate and Reichstag are surrounded by memorials of the murdered Jews in Europe, Soviet soldiers killed during WWII and of the victims of the Wall.

9

Berlin's Modern City Centre

Berlin central station

Federal chancellery

If you look at Berlin's modern city centre today, you should also take a look back into its past. A high-security prohibited area used to go that went so deep into East Berlin that any construction was made impossible. In the West of the city – a park landscape, which ended at the Wall, with a Reichstag that had been renovated in a rather makeshift fashion, and a lot of urban waste land no one knew or cared quite what to do with. Only the "bypass" route cut through the Eastern part of the Tiergarten park to make the journey between Kreuzberg and Wedding shorter and quicker, reminded West Berliners every time they took this road that there was another city behind the Wall and the Brandenburg Gate.

When West Berlin realised it could not boast of a cultural centre - unlike the East part of the city - construction of the Kulturforum was started 1960. WWII was not the only factor providing open space - in 1938, the former residential and administration district was

▲ Bellevue Palace

demolished to make way for the monumental "Great Germania" that Adolf Hitler and his "Generalbauinspekteur für die Reichshauptstadt Berlin" (General Building Inspector of the Reich Capital Berlin), Albert Speer had in mind.

Construction of the Kulturforum lasted decades and followed a general plan of the Architect Hans Scharoun. First the Philharmonie (1963), then the Neue Nationalgalerie (New National Gallery - 1968), the Staatsbibliothek (National Library - 1976), the Musikinstrumentenmuseum (Museum of Musical Instruments - 1984), the Kunstgewerbemuseum (Arts and Crafts Museum - 1985), the Kammermusiksaal (Chamber Music Hall -1987), the Kunstbibliothek (Arts Library) with its Copper Engraving Cabinet (1993) and lastly the Gemäldegalerie (Picture Gallery - 1997).

But at that point, the old plans had already been outstripped by the course of history. On the eastern outskirts of the Tiergarten, the construction of what is justifiably described as Berlin's modern city centre is already nearly complete.

▼ The House of World Cultures, formerly the Kongresshalle (Congress Hall)

"The Golden Else" on top of the Victory Column

11

▲ Neue Nationalgalerie and St. Matthäus

This includes the architectural constructions around Pariser Platz, the buildings of the Federation around the Reichstag, whose interior was completely converted, as well as the glassy central station, which replaced the old Lehrter Bahnhof building. The former bypass route, which used to run at ground level, was replaced by a tunnel connecting Potsdamer Platz with the central station. Also parts of the tunnel network for a new underground railway line – derisively called "Kanzler-linie" (Chancellor's line) by Berliners – have already been dug. The line is intended to connect Alexanderplatz with the central station; when the first trains will run here, however, is as yet unclear.

Also the older buildings which have long been lacking a good connection with the city quarters, will profit from this urbanistic development on the eastern outskirts of the Tiergarten.

View of Potsdamer Platz with the National Library

▲ Philharmonics ▼ Tiergarten with the Federal Chancellery ▲ Hamburger railway station

For example, the Bellevue Palace, built in 1785, the seat of the Federal President; the Kongresshalle (Congress Hall), opened in 1957 on the occasion of the International Construction Exhibition, today known as "Haus der Kulturen der Welt" (House of World Cultures); and the Hamburger Bahnhof, built 1846/47, the oldest station building in Berlin that is still preserved in its main parts. In 1885, it was decommissioned and now houses the "Museum für Gegenwart" (Museum for the Present).

People say that democracy itself was the constructor of the new buildings and their extensions in the government district. That is more just a nice image, it is true. Never before throughout German history has a government district looked less like fortress. In the Reichstag, people can look down on their parliament whenever they want. When and where has that ever been possible?

Potsdamer Platz – a Monument of the Future

Potsdamer Platz has never actually been a "Platz" (square). It got its name in 1831 to fit in with the Potsdamer Tor (Potsdam Gate), which had been erected on the Western edge of the nearby Leipziger Platz to plans by Karl Friedrich Schinkel. But even then it was only a big intersection, and in 1838, Potsdamer Bahnhof - the first station in the city- was built here. Around ninety years later, this place saw the biggest volume of traffic in Europe. The business and entertainment district was massively crowded. At the end of the Second World War the

square seemed deserted and eventually, after the construction of the Berlin Wall, it seemed completely dead: nothing remained but a barren expanse of space with elaborate border posts.

It took more than ten years after the reunification of East and West Berlin to revive the square and the nearby Kulturforum to a new and different kind of life. Nowadays, activity is no longer predominantly at ground level, but also in the multi-storied office blocks. They now characterise the area with their modern, sky-scraping architecture, which does not hide the fact that it is oriented around US standards – even if buildings there now reach even further into the sky.

▲ Beisheim-Center and DB-Tower ▼ Debis Skyscraper

Unter den Linden

▲ State Opera House　　▼ St. Hedwig's-Cathedral　　▲ Hotel Adlon

At one end: Pariser Platz with the Brandenburg Gate, at the other end: the long gone Berliner Schloss (Berlin City Palace) and the recently demolished Palast der Republik (Palace of the Republic). In between: the glamorous boulevard Unter den Linden, 60 metres wide – unusual even for Berlin – with an overall length of 1.5 kilometres.

The boulevard is almost an exhibition of the continuous gain of power Prussia and its Kings experienced between the late 17th Century and the proclamation of the Republic in 1918.

The avenue's predecessor was the riding and hunting path created by the Elector Johann Georg in 1573, which led from the Berliner Stadtschloss (Berlin City Palace) to the Elector's Tiergarten that he had created in the Western part of the city in 1527. The Great Elector Frederick-William ordered the paving of the riding path in 1647 and had linden and nut trees planted on its sides (along a stretch of 942 metres) according to Dutch custom. However, in the area of what today is Bebelplatz, many trees soon had to make way for new fortresses – and that has stayed the same to this today: even today, linden trees only line the Western part of the street between Universitätsstraße and Wilhelmstraße at Pariser Platz.

After the construction of the Zeughaus (today the Deutsches Historisches Museum – German History Museum), which had already started in 1687, Frederick II strongly promoted the cultivation of the eastern part of the boulevard. Hence, building works for the Forum Fridericianum commenced in 1740. It includes the Opera House, St. Hedwig's Cathedral, the Alte Bibliothek (Old Library) and, on the opposite side of the street, the Prinz-Heinrich-Palais, which belongs to the Humboldt University today.

After the victory over Napoleon in the Wars of Liberation, Frederick William III planned to extend the boulevard into a festive "Via triumphalis" with the help of his main builder Karl Friedrich Schinkel. But practical circumstances somehow downsized his plan: the monuments of Generals Scharnhorst and v. Bülow were erected as well as the Neue Wache (New Guard-House) and the Schlossbrücke (Palace Bridge). In addition, Christian Rauch's equestrian statue of Frederick the Great was placed on the central promenade near the present-day Bebelplatz in 1851.

▲ Prinzessinenpalais

▲ Humboldt-University

▲ former Town Major Bertelsmann House and Friedrichwerdersche Church

▲ Kronprinzenpalais   ▼ Neue Wache

The architectural monuments from feudal times also include the former Singakademie (Singing Academy), today the Maxim Gorky Theatre, the Palais am Festungsgraben (Palace by the Fortress Moat), the Kronprinzenpalais (Crown Prince Palace) and the Staatsbibliothek (National Library).

The western part of the boulevard Unter den Linden was for the most part rebuilt after the Second World War, and particularly attracts visitors to the city to take a stroll under the thick roof of leaves along its wide central promenade and take in the

▼ Alte Bibliothek, commode

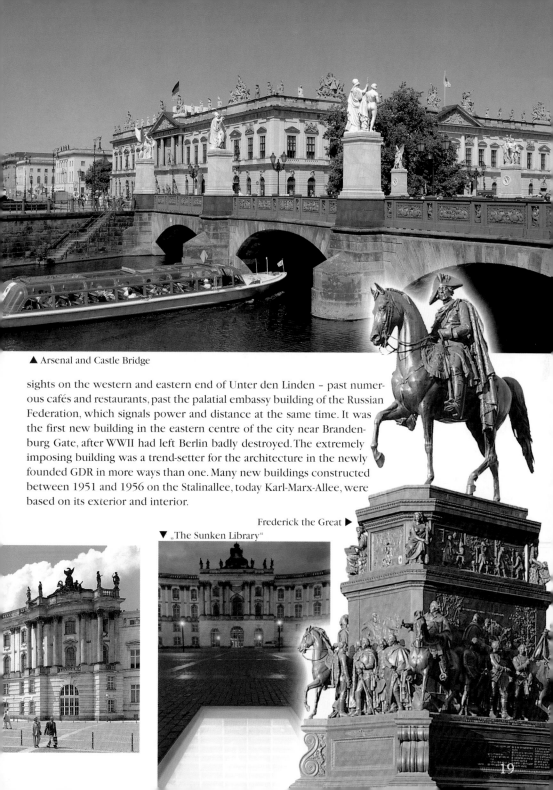

▲ Arsenal and Castle Bridge

sights on the western and eastern end of Unter den Linden – past numerous cafés and restaurants, past the palatial embassy building of the Russian Federation, which signals power and distance at the same time. It was the first new building in the eastern centre of the city near Brandenburg Gate, after WWII had left Berlin badly destroyed. The extremely imposing building was a trend-setter for the architecture in the newly founded GDR in more ways than one. Many new buildings constructed between 1951 and 1956 on the Stalinallee, today Karl-Marx-Allee, were based on its exterior and interior.

Frederick the Great ▶

▼ „The Sunken Library"

Museumsinsel –
the Museum Island

The construction of the museum island started with the Altes Museum (Old Museum) at Lustgarten. It was built between 1825 and 1830 to plans by Karl Friedrich Schinkel. With this museum, which was built at roughly the same time as the Glyptothek in Munich, Schinkel created the prototype of a civil museum; it was a type of building that was to greatly influence European museum architecture during the post-war era.

The idea to create a giant museum complex at the northern end of the river island between Kupfergraben and Spree goes back to suggestions by Prussian Crown Prince Frederick William, later to became Frederick William IV, who wanted to construct a "rich sanctuary for the arts and science" here, in keeping with the romantic mood of his time. He wanted to include institutes of the University Unter den Linden – formerly

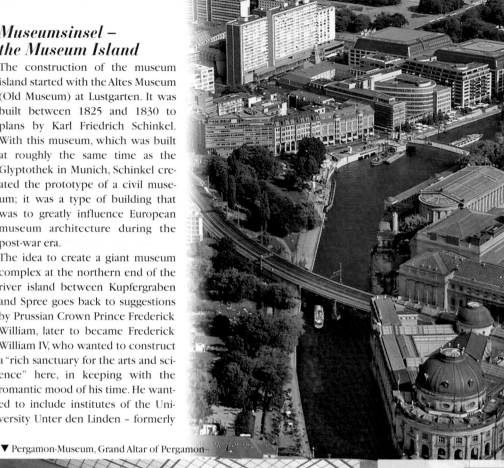

▼ Pergamon-Museum, Grand Altar of Pergamon

▲ Pergamon-Altar (Detail)

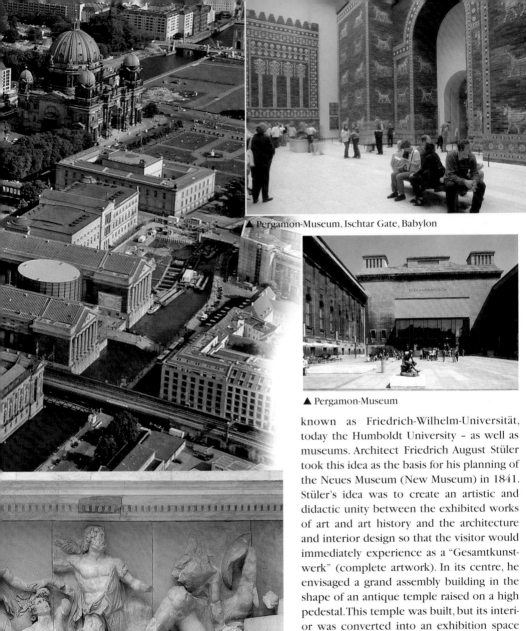

▲ Pergamon-Museum, Ischtar Gate, Babylon

▲ Pergamon-Museum

known as Friedrich-Wilhelm-Universität, today the Humboldt University – as well as museums. Architect Friedrich August Stüler took this idea as the basis for his planning of the Neues Museum (New Museum) in 1841. Stüler's idea was to create an artistic and didactic unity between the exhibited works of art and art history and the architecture and interior design so that the visitor would immediately experience as a "Gesamtkunstwerk" (complete artwork). In its centre, he envisaged a grand assembly building in the shape of an antique temple raised on a high pedestal. This temple was built, but its interior was converted into an exhibition space for contemporary arts showcasing the German art of the time: the assembly building was turned into the National Gallery, today called Alte Nationalgalerie (Old National Gallery). The neighbouring New Museum, which was renovated between 1986 and 2009, is connected with the Old National

21

▲ Bode-Museum

▲ Bode-Museum

Gallery by a circumferential, antique-like colonnade, which highlights the resulting museum complex as a special cultural area distinct from day-to-day urban life. The equestrian statue of King Frederick William IV on the outside staircase of the Alte Nationalgalerie reminds visitors of the intellectual creator of this architectural idea deeply embedded in the German Romantic age.

When Berlin's museums were suddenly able to make extensive new purchases at the end of the 19th century and to sponsor costly archaeological excavations, the existing museum space quickly became insufficient.

So the Kaiser-Friedrich-Museum (Emperor Frederick Museum), today called Bode Muse-

▲ Alte Nationalgalerie   ▼ Altes Museum

▲ Bode-Museum

▲ Adolph v. Menzel "Flute Concert", Alte Nationalgalerie

▲ hist. View castlke and cathedral

um was built during the years 1897–1904 to the north of the city railway constructed 1875–1882, on the tip of the museum island. The last complex on the museum island for the time being, the Pergamon Museum, was constructed between 1909 and 1930. Its long building phase can be explained by the difficult process of creating a steady foundation in the swampy ground, interruptions due to war and crises as well as disputes on cultural policy issues.

In September 1939, at the beginning of WW II, the institutions of the Museum Island were closed down like all museums in Berlin. The collections were packed up and stored in safe places. That is why relatively few works of art were actually destroyed during the War, while 80 percent of the buildings were demolished. Afterwards, it took a long time before the collections could be shown again in their original settings again. The Old National Gallery opened as first museum some rooms in June 1949, and from 1950 parts of the Pergamon and Bode Museum were again accessible, while reconstruction and restoration work on the Old Museum lasted until 1982. After elaborate restoration work, the New Museum has been opened again for visitors since the end of 2009.

◄ „Nofretete", Neues Museum

23

Berliner Dom – Berlin Cathedral

▲ Emperor's staircase ▼ Cathedral ▲ Sauer-Orgel

▲ Grand coffin of Frederick I.

▲ Choir

One could see it as a very strongly developed example of the tolerance that Berlin is famous for. Yet it is unusual that a Protestant cathedral is situated adjacent to the Lustgarten (Pleasure Garden). One cannot be sure what was here first. The Berliner Dom was erected at the location of the original church of a Dominican monastery, founded in 1297. Its hall was put together with the castle chapel to make up the cathedral chapter in the middle of the 16th century. Round about the same time, the Elector Johann Georg ordered the creation of a kitchen garden in the swamp area. However, it soon overgrew and was only redesigned into a Lustgarten by the Great Elector in the middle of the 17th century. Under the rule of the "Soldier King" Frederick William I, the pleasures had to make way for a parade ground. From 1745-50, a Protestant cathedral was built, which replaced the Dominican church. Between 1816 and 1820 this cathedral was redecorated in Classical style by Schinkel. But in 1893, it had been already torn down again and the Berliner Dom was erected as a neo-Baroque colossus from 1893 to 1905. Since that time, it has served as the main church of Prussian Protestantism and as the chapel royal and memorial church of the Hohenzollern dynasty. The sacred building was huge: 114 metres long, 77 metres wide and 114 metres high, up to the cross on its dome, with a capacity for 4,500 people in the dome area. During the Second World War, the dome itself was heavily damaged and restored starting in 1975. This process led to the reduction of the dome and spiral endings - to 98 metres up to the tip of cross in the dome -, the interior and exterior structure was simplified and the former mausoleum on the north front was not reconstructed.

▲ Deutscher Dom, Schauspielhaus and Französischer Dom

Many people consider the Gendarmenmarkt the most beautiful square in Berlin. It is definitely the most important ensemble of historically valuable buildings in the city centre. Extended over a period of approx. 120 years, the wide square with the two cathedrals and the central Schauspielhaus (Playhouse) seems like one flawless piece. The square was created as a market square towards the end of the 17th century, following the extension of Friedrichstadt. In 1799, it was named after the cuirassier regiment "Gens d'Armes", the armed bodyguards of the King. It only got the appearance that we still see today in 1821 with the completion of the Schauspielhaus designed by Karl Friedrich Schinkel. Today, it serves as a concert hall. At that time, the two magnificent corresponding towers of the Deutscher Dom (German Cathedral) in the south and the Französischer Dom (French Cathedral) in the north, had already stood there

▲ Galeries Lafayette Department Store

▲ Quartier 206

for a 36 years. The Schiller monument is the work of the Sculptor Reinhold Begas. It was ceremoniously unveiled on November 10, the 112th birthday of the Poet.

During the Second World War, the ensemble was badly damaged. Long-term reconstruction works commenced towards the end of the 1970s. But it will never be finished – there was something that needs to be renovated.

The 3.3-km-long Friedrichstraße runs parallel to the Gendarmenmarkt from north to south. With department stores like the Galeries Lafayette and Quartier 205 and 206, it is getting more and more attractive. At least during the daytime, this boulevard is full of vibrancy between Leipziger Straße and Friedrichstraße station.

Schauspielhaus, today the Konzerthaus (Concert Hall) ▲

▼ Atrium of Quartiers 206

The Nikolai district

▲ St. Nikolai

The Nikolai district is an urbanistic piece of art from GDR times. If you don't look too closely, you might find it resembles Berlin's old town, which was to a large extent destroyed during WWII, before most of it was removed. But it is not like that. It only looks like it in parts.

What you see here was built on the historic urbanistic rota of the former district between 1979 and 1987. Also buildings that carried some importance in Berlin,

St. Georg the Dragon Slayer ▶

▲ "Zum Nußbaum"

▲ At the riverbanks of the Spree

▲ Ephraim-Palais

but which stood somewhere else, were quickly integrated, e.g. the guesthouse "Zum Nußbaum", or a replica of the Gerichtslaube – the original stands in Babelsberg Park in Potsdam – as well as the sculpture of the dragonslayer, which used to stand in the Stadtschloss.

▲ Bärenzwinger-Brunnen (Bear-Pit Fountain)

Under the TV Tower

▲ St. Marien

The park-like green space stretching from the river Spree via the Marx-Engels-Forum all the way to the TV tower, is owing to the destruction of WWII. Before the war that space used to be densely built up, but only the two buildings remaining in the district from the pre-war period are the Protestant parish church St. Marien, whose origin can be traced back to the early 13th century, and opposite it, the Rathaus (Town Hall) of Berlin, also called the "Rotes Rathaus" (Red Town Hall) – which has nothing to do with the political colouring of the rulers.

Between the Town Hall and the church, you can

The TV tower sticks out into the sky far beyond all other buildings in Berlin, like a giant exclamation mark: this is Berlin, this is the heart of Berlin. The delicate construction, which is 368m high today – after the antenna was elongated several times – has a paned tower dome at 207m, which houses a café that rests on a circulating ring. If you are lucky enough to get a seat in the café, you will have the chance to see the entire city from a bird's eye perspective in half an hour. That is the duration of one whole round.

▼ Neptune Fountain in front of the "Rotes Haus" (Red Town Hall)

now find the Neptune fountain, which used to be situated on the southern forecourt of the City Castle. This powerful, buoyant fountain was conceived in the workshop of the sculptor Reinhold Begas in 1891.

Alexanderplatz, a few steps down the railway line, comes across less opulently. It received its current appearance during the extension of the East Berlin city centre between 1966 and 1970. The decorative elements on this three-hectare square, which is used to having some heavy winds whistling through every nook and cranny, have survived: the Weltzeituhr (World Time Clock) and the fountain.

31

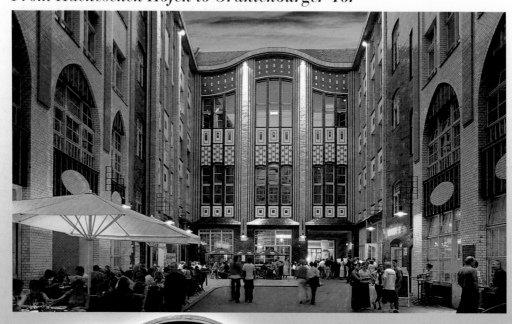

In the summer, the northern station forecourt at Hackescher Markt marks the beginning of a whole chain of street cafés, stretching through Oranienburger Straße all the way to Friedrichstraße, where the Oranienburger Tor (Oranienburg Gate) used to stand, and where the still rather derelict-looking arts centre Tacheles in a former department store building attracts the curious and brave.

The Hackesche Höfe were named after Hans Christoph Friedrich Count von Hacke, who was appointed Military Commander of Berlin by Frederick II in 1749. They are a unique complex of 8 connected innercity residential, event and commercial units, with an overall space of 10,000 square meters. Built in 1906, the complex shows off its whole glory in courts decorated with colourful Art Nouveau brick facades.

▲ Tacheles   ▼ Sommer garden at Hackescher Markt Station

▼ Spree beach in Monbijou-Park

33

The Memorial to the Murdered Jews of Europe

▲ Memorial at Große Hamburger Straße

◀ Synagoge, Oranienburger Straße

▲ Jewish Museum ▼

The first documented proof of Jewish life in Berlin dates back to the 13th century. In 1671, the Elector Frederick William released an edict enabling displaced Jews from Vienna to settle in Brandenburg. On September 10, 1671 the first Austrian families received a charter of protection. This day is seen as the foundation day of the Jewish community of Berlin. But the first synagogue was only inaugurated in 1714. From then on, the number of Jews living in Berlin grew continuously. In 1925, the 172,672 Jews living in the city made up 4.3 percent of the overall population. This was around a fifth of all Jews living in the Weimar Republic at the time.

With Adolf Hitler's appointment as Reich Chancellor first started with the persecution, then the systematic murder of Jews in Germany was started, later also spreading to those countries Germany had occupied.

Today, numerous monuments, memorials and museums remind of the atrocities that the National Socialist state Jews of the city and throughout Europe. At the same time, Jews have regained ground and the Jewish community of Berlin once again numbers around 12,000 members. That nearly equals the number of Jews who lived in the city in the middle of the 19th century.

The Berlin Wall

The barrier erected around the Western sectors of Berlin, which were put up as on August 13, 1961, were intended to put a stop to the increasing stream of refugees from the GDR. With that move, the GDR, supported by the Soviet Union and the other states of the Warsaw Pact, isolated West Berlin from its surroundings as much as possible. The facilities: at first wooden or barbed wire fences were further extended in the following years and developed into a massive construction, passable only through a few official transit points.

Of the 162 km of barricades, 37 km predominantly ran through residential areas, 17 km through industrial parks, 30 km through forested areas, 24 km through water, 54 km passed railway embankments or fields and swamp areas. The Wall stopped transit traffic on eight urban and four underground railway lines. It interrupted 192 main and side streets, 97 of which led into East Berlin and 95 into the GDR. In its final state, an approx. 4-m-high concrete wall spread over 107 km, a three to four meter high metal grate fence stretched across 65 km. Some places even had both constructions. 300 watch towers, 22 bunkers and 256 dog pens ensured the safeguarding of the border.

The Berlin Wall claimed numerous victims. The first was 47-year-old Rolf Urban, who died on August 19, 1961 during his attempt to absail from a building in Bernauer Straße, in the district of Wedding, onto the West Berlin pavement. The last two victims of a total of 80 deaths that occurred during attempted passage

▼ Potsdamer Platz vor 1989

to West Berlin, were 20-year-old Chris Gueffroy, who was shot during his attempt in Treptow in the night of February 6, 1989, and 32-year-old Winfried Freundenberg, who crashed above Zehlendorf in a self-built hot-air balloon on March 8, 1989. Little remains of the former Wall: there are only 13 places in the city area where one can still see small parts of it in varying degrees of preservation. In order to not let this monstrous construction, which divided a whole city from one day to the next completely sink into oblivion the Berlin Senate initiated the creation of so-called "Orte der Erinnerung" (Places of Remembrance) at eight places along the inner-city route of the Wall: in the Mauerpark (Wall Park), on the area of the Nordbahn at Bernauer Straße, in the Invalidenpark, at the Tränenpalast in front of Friedrichstraße station, at the Reichstag, in Niederkirchnerstraße, at Checkpoint Charlie and at the East-Side Gallery.

Die Mauer 1961–1989

Grenze West-/Ost-Berlin

Grenzübergänge
1 Bornholmer Straße
2 Chausseestraße
3 Invalidenstraße
4 Friedrichstraße
  Checkpoint Charlie
5 Heinrich-Heine-Straße
6 Oberbaumbrücke
7 Sonnenallee

Reinickendorf · Pankow · Hohenschönhausen · Weißensee · Wedding · Prenzlauerberg · Spandau · Tiergarten · MITTE · Friedrichshain · Marzahn · Charlottenburg · Kreuzberg · Lichtenberg · Hellersdorf · Wilmersdorf · Schöneberg · Zehlendorf · Steglitz · Tempelhof · Neukölln · Treptow · Köpenick

▲ GI meets Volkspolizist ▲ Checkpoint Charlie in the old days ..... ▼ ..... and today

The construction of the "Socialist Wall of Protection" began in the early morning of August 13. During the night of November 9, 1989, this "protective wall" did not exactly fall, but suddenly became penetrable in both directions. Most people could not quite believe it at first. Hardly anyone among the citizens passing through this border themselves that night – a border, which had once seemed completely impenetrable – could have guessed that the relations between the two German states were so seriously unhinged by this day, which bore such historical significance.

The night the Wall fell has become history. We are reminded of it by tradesmen selling devotional objects and socialist insignia at tourist places and – maybe less exciting and busy – by the Gedenkstätte Berliner Mauer (Berlin Wall Memorial) at Bernauer Straße, which was created on the former death strip to give visitors an impression of what it used to be like around the Wall until November 9, 1989: very quiet and very ominous.

▲ The Berlin Wall, with holes, but still watched over, ...

▲ ... then people start streaming through Brandenburg Gate ...

▲ ... and first occuping the Wall with satisfaction ...

▲ ... before watching its demolition contentedly.

▲ The Berlin Wall Memorial at Bernauer Straße

Friedrichshain and Treptow

▲ East-Side-Gallery

The bridge Oberbaumbrücke connects the two districts Kreuzberg and Friedrichshain, which now belong to the same part of the city. During the Cold War, the river Spree also served as a border between East and West Berlin at this point. A relic from this time is the East-Side Gallery, a 1,300m section of the Wall in Mühlenstraße between Ostbahnhof and Oberbaumbrücke, adorned with very different types of graffiti by 118 artists from 21 states. On the opposite side of the street, a giant shopping and entertainment park is under construction, featuring o2

▲ o2 World

▼ East-Side-Gallery

▲ Molecule Men

World, a great sport and mutifunctional hall of the Anschutz Entertainment Group.

The 30-m-high sculpture "Molecule Men" by the US Artist Jonathan Borofsky in the river Spree does not only serve decorative purposes for onlooking Treptowers on the embankment. The three figures also symbolise the districts Friedrichshain, Kreuzberg and Treptow, which meet at this point. With Treptower Park and Plänterwald, Treptow presents its giant leisure and entertainment facilities here. At the centre of the park, you find a memorial of the Red Army in remembrance of those Soviet soldiers who died during the battle of Berlin.

◄ Soviet Cenotaph Treptow ▲

41

Between Wittenbergplatz and Breitscheidplatz

Tauentzienstraße near Breitscheidplatz – with the Kaiser-William-Gedächtniskirche at one end and the glamorous department store Kaufhaus des Westens, or KaDeWe for short, at the other end – is Berlin's shopping mile, even if this wide boulevard is only 450 m long.

The street is named after the Prussian General Tauentzien von Wittenberg and was only constructed in the second half of the 19th century. At first it led through cornfields and garden centres. From 1880 onwards, more and more noble residences were added. The character of this peaceful residential street changed promptly, when shopping mogul A. Jandorf engaged Emil Schaudt to set up his giant department store complex KaDeWe here in 1907, adjacent to the 280 x 140 m square Wittenbergplatz. This had the result that more and more shops

▲ Breitscheidplatz ▼ "Wasserklops" (Water Dumpling)

▼ Wittenbergplatz and the KaDeWe

opening along in the formerly residential street. Today "der Tauentzien", as Berliners say, is a shopping mile for upmarket requirements. It features the monumental gate sculpture "Berlin" by Brigitte and Martin Matschinsky-Denninghoff in a big flowerbed on the centre strip. It was put up for the occasion of the 750-year anniversary of the city in 1987.

The eastern end of Tauentzienstraße is marked by the Europa Center, built in 1963/65 and frequently altered since then. It stands on the spot where the Romanische Café used to be, that famous meeting place of littérateurs and artists in the first decade of the Weimar Republic.

In front of the Europa Center lies the vehicle-free Breitscheid-Platz with the fountain "Weltkreisbrunnen" designed by Joachim Schmettau in 1983, and the Kaiser-William-Gedächtniskirche (Emperor William Memorial Church) with its annexes built between 1959 and 1961 to plans by Egon Eier-

mann. The Gedächtniskirche, which was originally intended for the Wittenbergplatz, was inaugurated in 1895 and badly damaged during WWII. In the 1950s, there were vehement public discussions about whether the church should be demolished and completely rebuilt at a different spot or whether the 68m spiral ruin should be preserved – originally, the main spiral had had a height of 113m. After a competition, it was decided to leave the ruin as it was and surround it with the new constructions we see today (nave, foyer, wedding chapel and baptistery as well as the tower).

▼ Gedächtnishalle (Memorial Hall) with mosaics and marble reliefs

▼ Tauentzienstraße

Kurfürstendamm – Ku'damm

▲ Kranzler Eck

The Ku'damm, or actually Kurfürsten-
damm, is like a 3.5 km green ribbon that
runs through the city from Breitscheid-
Platz all the way to Halensee. It was constructed in 1886 on the initiative of the former Reich Chancellor von Bismarck instead
of a log causeway. Until the early 1990s, the
boulevard was the centre of West Berlin's glitzy
world. Among numerous luxury boutiques, one
could also find Currywurst stalls, cafés, restaurants,
(cabaret) theatres, cinemas, and other entertainment
facilities galore. This has changed. Ku'damm, or
"City-West" as it is called nowadays, is no longer the
indisputable centre of Berlin. It has become quieter
again, but also more beautiful and laid-back.

▼ Theater des Westens

▲ Ku'damm-Eck   ▼ Zoo

45

Charlottenburg Palace

When the construction of Charlottenburg Palace started in the last decade of the 17th century, it was intended as a summer residence or maybe a pleasure palace for the Electoral Princess of Brandenburg, Sophie-Charlotte. Back in those days, no one could guess what Charlottenburg would one day become. The building site was far out of the city, but was still directly accessible from the City Palace: Straight on, past the Großer Stern, past what today is Ernst-Reuter-Platz, then along the Bismarckstraße, to Schlossstraße, a grove that has long been able to boast of four rows of trees leads directly to the steps of the palace.

The palace was intended as a gift from Elector Frederick III, later the first King of Prussia, Frederick I, to his wife. But she died in 1705 – the palace's name pays homage to her – without ever getting a glimpse of the completed palace nor the Château Park in its present-day appearance. Even Frederick I, who died in 1713, only ever saw rudiments of the entire complex.

This was because the castle and its park remained one big building site until the middle of the 19th century. Despite many the different master

▲ Equestrain Statue of the Great Elector

builders – Nehring, Eosander, Knobelsdorff, Langhans, Gentz and Schinkel – despite various garden and landscape planners – Godeau, Eyerbeck and Lenné – it still turned out a Baroque complex of captivating beauty.

One can best take in the full beauty and diversity of the Château Park from above: in the north, towards the urban railway line, one finds the artistic instinctiveness of an English landscape garden, where swinging paths cross picturesque little streams, small hills offer great vistas and meadows invite weary visitors to rest awhile among old trees.

47

▲ Schinkel's Neuer Pavillon (Neuer Pavilion)

▲ Mausoleum

In the south, towards the stretched palace building, one finds the strict geometrics of a French garden with an octagonal fountain pool at its centre and linden avenues offering shelter from sun and rain.

A definite must-see is the Belvedere on the outer rim of the château garden. It was built by Carl Gotthard Langhans during the years 1788 to 1790. The small, pretty building used to stand on a small river island in the Spree, where it was used as a tea pavilion and watchtower. Today it houses a collection of Berlin porcelain from the 18th and 19th century, predominantly works by the Königliche Porzellanmanufaktur (Royal Porcelain Manufacturers – KPM).

The mausoleum in the western park area is also worth a visit. It was erected as a burial place for Queen Luise between 1810 and 1812 and features the cenotaphs of Queen Luise and King Frederick William III, made to plans by Christian Daniel Rauch, as well as the cenotaphs of the Emperor William I and Empress Augusta, both works by Erdmann Encke.

▲ Belvedere

▲ Porcelain cabinet in the palace

East of the Knobelsdorff wing lies the Neue Pavillon by Karl-Frederick Schinkel, built in 1824/1825 on a nearly perfectly square floor plan in strict formation. In front of this, you see two granite pillars with sculptures of two very lively goddesses of victory, designed by Christian Daniel Rauch in 1840.

Prinzessinnengruppe (Group ▶ of Princesses) by Gottfried v. Schadow Luise and Friederike

49

Museums in Berlin

If you want to visit all the museums in Berlin, you have to come equipped with a lot of time, money and endurance. Berlin offers access to nearly 160 museums and collections. This includes everything from A, the "Abgusssammlung antiker Plastik" (Cast collection of antique sculptures) in Charlottenburg's Schlossstraße, to Z, the "Zucker-Museum" (Sugar Museum) in Amrumer Straße in the district of Wedding. The number of private galleries and collections is also enormous.

The museums collect, document and offer the public scientific insights into nearly all areas of art and art history, natural history and technology as well as general history. In addition, there are numerous memorials and monuments, which draw a connection between past and present.

Deutsches Technikmuseum
◀ (German Technology Museum)

▲ DDR-Museum (GDR Museum)

Berlin's museums are distributed over the entire city. The most important are concentrated at three locations: the Museum Island in the centre of Berlin (Old National Gallery, Old Museum, Bode Museum, Pergamon Museum, Märkisches Museum and New Museum), the Cultural Forum on the periphery of the Tiergarten and Potsdamer Platz (New National Gallery, Picture Gallery, Art Library, Arts and Crafts Museum,

◀ Museum für Naturkunde (Natural History Museum)

▲ Deutsches Historisches Museum (German History Museum) ▶
with an annex by Ieoh Ming Pei

▼ Museumszentrum Dahlem

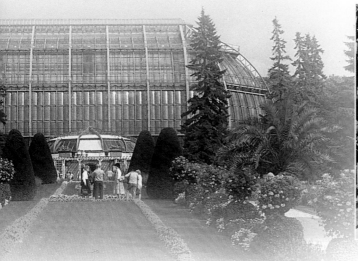

▲ Botanicel Gardens

Musical Instrument Museum, State Library and German Technology Museum) and the Museum Centre in Dahlem (Museum for Indian Art, Museum for East Asian Art, Ethnological Museum for African art with North America exhibition, Museum of European Cultures).

Martin-Gropius-Building ▶

"In the posh West"

▲ Bell tower on Maifeld

In all continental cities of Europe, the western districts are more upmarket, while poor people live mostly in the east closer to the factories. The reason is simple: as continents mostly have westerly winds, the air is best in the western districts and the smut from factory chimneys does not pollute the city but the hinterland.

It is no different in Berlin. A privileged neighbourhood lies west of the circle line and the city ring road, between Heerstraße and Spandauer Damm. Its nothern part, the elegant residential area Westend, was founded in 1866. Many villas and country homes have survived from the Gründerzeit period and the following decades. On its southern borders lies the so-called Neu-Westend. Since 1910, a lot of well-fitted single and multi-family houses were built here.

Numerous impressive sights lie around this elegant residential district. This includes the Haus des Rundfunks (House of Broadcasting) on Masurenallee – built to designs by Hans Poelzig in 1929/30 – with a structured brickwork facade and a foyer spanning across five stories.

Right on the opposite side of the road lies the entrance to Berlin's exhibition grounds, the Messegelände, which has been expanded several times over the past decades. It also includes the

▼ Waldbühne

▲ In Olympic Stadium

▲ Radio tower and International Congress Center

International Congress Center (ICC). The Radio Tower protrudes high above the entire area; it is another landmark of Berlin. It was inaugurated with a speech by Albert Einstein in 1926.

Further west lies the Olympiastadion (Olympic Stadium), which was constructed between 1934 and 1936 along with the surrounding sports facilities – a swimming stadium, hockey stadium, the Deutsches Sportforum, a riding stadium, the Maifeld with its bell tower and the Waldbühne (Forest Stage). The Olympic Stadium was carefully renovated and extended on the occasion of the FIFA World Cup 2006 held in Germany and today meets the highest possible demands in the sporting arena.

Berlin – the Water City

▲ Zitadelle Spandau

Berlin is situated on the waterfront: five rivers run through the city, six channels serve as transport routes and 50 lakes offer relaxation and bathing opportunities. Indeed, one could say that nearly seven percent of the city area lies constantly under water. Berliners benefit from this enormously, thanks to the Müggelsee in

▲ Palace on the island Pfaueninsel

"Der Hauptmann von Köpenick" ("The Captain
◀ of Köpenick" – a play by Carl Zuckmayer)   ▼ Schloss Köpenick

▲ Lakes and forest: Havelseen and Grunewald

the east of the city as much as the Havelseen in the west; although strictly speaking the latter ones are actually not lakes, but expansions of the rivers Spree and Havel.

The lake embankments are lined with prominent and important buildings, which give an impressive testimony of the development of Berlin, after the first settlers arrived in the swampy meadows of the river Spree around 720.

▲ Grunewald Tower

▼ Glienicker Brigde – "The Bridge of the Spies"

Sanssouci Palace, Potsdam

Without its palaces and gardens, Potsdam would be a regional capital like any other and would attract little tourist interest. But Sanssouci Palace dominates this unique culture landscape. Georg Wenzeslaus Knobelsdorff created it for Frederick II, also called "Frederick the Great", or "Old Fritz". The flat, elongated building above the terraced vineyard has two faces: the court has a Classicist colonnade comprised of 88 Corinthian pillars. Standing here, you would not guess that the side facing the garden features an opulent and almost playful design. Very lively Rococo-style Baccus reliefs, with the figures stemming the flat pent roof in drunken nonchalance.

The court and garden front of the Palace are reconciliated in the interior, in the central Marble Hall. Here, the martial emblems in the dome vanish behind the four radiant white groups of figures on the cornice above the doors.

▲ Library　　　　　▼ Voltaire Room

Frederick ►
the Great

▼ Marbel Hall

The opulence of the Palace's sunny side is continued in the interior on both sides of the marble hall. The eastern side leads into the apartments of Frederick II, the other side takes you into five guest rooms, including the "Voltaire Room, which Voltaire never actually stayed in, having fled from the King long before the room was finished. He definitely missed out: colourful bushes, bouquets and garlands are set off against the light yellow wall panelling, which features such naturalistic images of many animals that you might think they have just fallen into a deep sleep. The King's rooms in the other wing are of opulent magnificence and suave elegance. In a cloud of celadon, the King's favourite colour, all artistic works are combined with workmanship tools to make up a big ensemble presented as one big "Gesamtkunstwerk", a complete artwork.

Sanssouci Park

▲ New Chambers and Historic Mill

has the small Classical Charlottenhof Palace(1829), designed by Karl Friedrich Schinkel in cooperation with the renowned landscape planner and gardener Peter Joseph Lenné, and the nearby Roman Baths dating back to 1835. Finally, on the northern edges of the park, there is the Orangery, which was completed in 1860. It was modelled on Italian architecture and its bulky length of 300 meters is a whole 60 meters longer than the Neues Palais (New Palace). The original sketches for this building were done by Frederick William

Frederick II called this construction a "fanfaronade", sheer ostentation. The interior is filled with trinkets: the beautiful Baroque theatre, still used as a theatre today, the giant ballroom and the opulently decorated Shell Hall.

But the park has more to offer than two very different palaces, about 800 meters apart. It also features the Great Fountain at the foot of Sanssouci Palace, the incredibly playful Chinesisches Haus (Chinese House - 1754) with its stone people in the loggia, turning the observer into a witness of all goings-on. It also

▼ Chinesisches Haus

IV. who died of mental confusion and a generous overdose of champagne in 1861. The Neue Kammern (new chambers) in the west seem almost like appendices to Sanssouci Palace (built in 1747). First they served as orangery, then as a guesthouse, and along with the Bildergalerie opposite them (1755), as one of the earliest art galleries worldwide.

The park with the Neues Palais (New Palace) on the western borders and the Communs (both from 1769) behind, is full of sights. The palace is as pretentious as it was expensive – and it was very expen-

▲ Orangery

sive. The palace has an overall length of 240 meters, it has 200 rooms and is adorned with 478 figures in front of and on the façade.

▼ Neues Palais, Marble Gallery

◀ Neues Palais
◀ Charlottenhof Palace
▼ Roman Baths

The town Potsdam

▲ Nauen Gate   ▼ Jägertor (Hunter's Gate)

▼ Brandenburg Gate

▼ Alexandrowka ▲ Old Market Square with Nikolaikirche

▲ Royal Stables, Film Museum

▲ Former Town Hall

▲ "Lange Kerls"

Holländisches Viertel –
the Dutch Quarter ▶

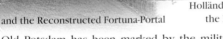

and the Reconstructed Fortuna-Portal

Old Potsdam has been marked by the military; in 1945 it was burned almost entirely to the ground by 490 British Royal Air Force bombers. After this, the historic centre around the palace and the Alter Markt (Old Town Square) did not exist anymore. Schinkel's Nikolaikirche (St. Nicholas's Church), the Altes Rathaus (Old Town Hall), a colonnade, which used to connect the palace with the royal stables, the obelisk and the then recently put up Fortuna-Portal. The different city gates at the edges of this formerly central square (The construction a building for the Brandenburg Parliament here is planned so as to give the square back some "shape") are surprising: the neo-gothic gates Nauener Tor (built 1754) and Brandenburger Tor (1770). Beyond Nauener Tor lies the former Russian colony Alexandrowka from 1827, on the other side the Holländisches Viertel (Dutch Quarter) from the year 1742.

New Garden and Babelsberg Palace

▲ Cecilienhof Palace

In the northeastern part of Potsdam, particularly in the Neuer Garten (New Garden), you find the last architectural highlights of the Prussian rulers and German Emperors, the Hohenzollern dynasty: the Marmorpalais (Marble Palace, built 1787-1844), Babelsberg Palace (1833-1849) and Cecilienhof Palace (1912-1917).

The Marmorpalais, which lies surrounded by a multitude of curious buildings in the Neuer Garten, served as a summer residence for Frederick William II. Babelsberg Palace was a gift to Prince William, who was to become the first Emperor of the German Reich, and Princess Augusta.

▼ Marmorpalais (Marble Palace) at Heiliger See

▲ King Frederick William II.

Cecilienhof Palace ▶

▲ Conference Hall, Cecilienhof Palace

▲ Potsdamer Conference 1945

try mansion. The interior design is dominated by comfort and tastefulness. After the end of the Second World War, the Heads of State of the Allied victorious powers met here in the summer of 1945 for the Potsdam Conference, – Germany's borders were redrawn, Berlin became a 4-sector city, all of Germany was divided into 4 occupied sectors, Prussia as a state ceased to exist. This was done by Truman for the USA, Stalin for the USSR and first Churchill, then Attlee for Great Britain. Germany's division was sealed – until 1989 – who could have guessed that at the time?

Cecilienhof Palace takes on a special position. During the First World War, from 1914–17, it was built as a residence for the royal couple Crown Prince William (1882–1951) and his wife, Cecilie von Mecklenburg-Schwerin (1886–1954). The complex has 176 rooms and adopted the style of an English coun-

Babelsberg Palace

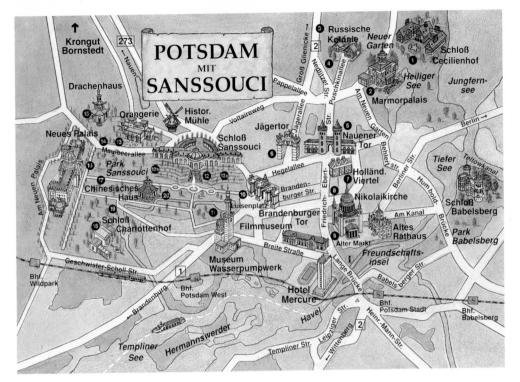

Sight in Potsdam

1. Cecilienhof Palace, 1913–17
2. Marmorpalais, built 1787–91
3. Belvedere on the hill Pfingstberg, 1843–52 and 1860–62
4. Russian Colony Alexandrowka from 1826 with Russian-Orthodox Church from 1829
5. Nauener Tor, built 1755
6. Jägertor, built 1733
7. Holländisches Viertel – The Dutch Quarter
8. Peter- u. Pauls-Kirche, built on Bassinplatz from 1867–70 and French Church from 1752
9. Alter Markt (Old Town Square) with Nikolakirche, built 1830–37, the Altes Rathaus (OldTown Hall), built 1753–55 and Knobelsdorffhaus
10. Brandenburger Tor, built at Luisenplatz, 1770
11. Friedenskirche (Peace Church) in the Marly-Garten, built 1845–54
12. Sanssouci Palace,1745–47 (extended 1841–42), with vineyard terraces and the Great Fountain
12.a Neptune grotto from 1751–57 a. Art Gallery, built 1755–64

12.b New Chambers, built 1747 (extended 1771–74) and the Historic Mill of Sanssouci from 1790
13. Orangery, built 1851–60, with Jubilee Terrace a. Hofgärtnerhaus (Court Gardener's House)
14. Botanical Gardens a. Botanical Institute
15. Drachenhaus from 1770 a. Belvedere from 1770–72
16. Neues Palais, built 1763–69 with the Communs beyond, built 1766–69 in an elaborate, representative style. They served as outbuildings and for domestic staff and the royal entourage.
17. Freundschaftstempel (Friendship Temple) from 1770 and Antikentempel (Antique Temple) from 1769
18. Charlottenhof Palace, built 1826–29
19. Roman Baths and Court Gardener's House), built from 1829
20. Chinesisches Teehaus (Chinese Tea Pavilion), built 1754–57.